OFF WE GO!
TO CHENNAI, TO CHENNAI

TALKING CUB
Speaking Tiger Publishing Pvt. Ltd
4381/4 Ansari Road, Daryaganj, New Delhi – 110002, India

Published in Talking Cub, an imprint of Speaking Tiger, in association with INTACH in hardback in 2020

Text and illustrations copyright © INTACH 2020

ISBN: 978-93-90477-85-2
eISBN: 978-93-90477-84-5

10 9 8 7 6 5 4 3 2 1

Designed by Aniruddha Mukherjee for Syllables27, a specialised children's content outfit run by the authors to produce books for children on a turn-key basis for various publishers and organisations.

All rights reserved.
No part of this publication may be reproduced, transmitted, or stored in a retrieval system, in any form or by any means, electronic, mechanical, photocopying, recording or otherwise, without the prior permission of the publisher.

This book is sold subject to the condition that it shall not, by way of trade or otherwise, be lent, resold, hired out, or otherwise circulated, without the publisher's prior consent, in any form of binding or cover other than that in which it is published.

OFF WE GO!
TO CHENNAI TO CHENNAI

WRITTEN BY ARTHY MUTHANNA SINGH AND MAMTA NAINY
ILLUSTRATED BY VIBHA SURYA

I love it when my mother massages coconut oil in my hair. One, I love the aroma of coconut in any form and two, Amma always hums or sings while she makes sure that every strand of hair on my head is almost soaked from end to end. My hair has grown right down till my waist. It is such a bother when I play tennis, but it is great for Bharatanatyam. It can be decorated beautifully with jasmine flowers and hair ornaments.

JASMINE, THE QUEEN OF FLOWERS!

What a lovely fragrance it has! It is also called God's own flower because it is used for every festival. Women from Tamil Nadu like to wear jasmine flowers in their hair. Madurai malligai puu is the most famous and popular variety of jasmine.

In the hot summers of Chennai, my Amma helps me tie my hair in a knot right on top of my head, which is then made into a tight plait. I saw a photograph in Amma Paatti's, my grandmother's, home in Puducherry of my Amma Paatti and my Amma smiling, both with two thick plaits each, covered with jasmine flowers. They looked like sisters!

My Amma Paatti often says, 'Viji, I will come to Madras for Pongal.' Or, 'Madras is too hot in the summer, I will come in December.' She *never* says Chennai.

'Chennai, Paatti, Chennai,' I say. She just smiles.

MADRASPATNAM TO CHENNAI

It was only in January 1969 that Madras State was changed to Tamil Nadu. The name of the capital was changed from Madras to Chennai in 1996. It was called Madraspatnam much before that.

This December, everyone is coming to Chennai for Kamala Chithi's — my mother's younger sister's — wedding and my arangetram. Yay! New pavadai, new salwar kameez, new dance costume...so much fun.

All my first cousins, second cousins, my aunts, uncles, Paattis and Thathas will be here. My house will be full of relatives from all over the world. And the best part — Amma Paatti will be here with me for two full months before the wedding for shopping and planning.

Amma said we should show them all the lovely places in Chennai. We could go for a picnic, maybe.

ARANGETRAM

In Tamil 'arangam' means a stage and 'etram' means climbing. So, arangetram means climbing the stage for a debut performance of dance. It is the graduation ceremony when the guru presents his or her pupil to the public.

I start making a list. We cannot leave out the Crocodile Farm. I am sure none of my cousins have seen a crocodile up close. And, we have to go to Amma's college.

We live in Kotturpuram which is not very far from IIT Madras, where Amma goes to work. Amma is a Computer Science Professor. She has taken me to the campus many times. There are so many trees. Some parts of the campus look like a jungle! I saw deer there once, crossing the road. Maybe I too will study at IIT when I grow up...

Appa works at the MS Swaminathan Research Foundation at Taramani as a Marine Biologist, but I think he should have been a mridangam player. He is so good at playing that instrument! Sometimes when he has time, we do a jugalbandi. I dance and he plays the mridangam, slowly at first. Then he gets faster and faster, as I dance faster and faster, until I give up because we are both laughing so much!

My dance guru is Radha Akka. She is the best Bharatanatyam dancer in the whole world. She studied at Kalakshetra. She is so graceful and kind, but she can be strict sometimes. I don't know how she always knows when I have not practised. I hope I don't make any mistakes during my arangetram.

Radha Akka lives in Mylapore and a few months ago, she took all seven of us from the dance class to see the Kapaleeshwarar Temple there. She said it was one of the oldest temples in Chennai.

DID YOU KNOW?

Rukmini Devi Arundale was a famous Bharatanatyam dancer who set up an arts centre for music and dance, with the help of her husband Dr George Sydney Arundale and her brother Yagneswaran in January 1936. It was the International Centre for Arts in the campus of the Theosophical Society. There was a lot of support from their mentor Dr Annie Besant. It was later named Kalakshetra and is now in Besant Nagar. Rukmini was the first woman to be nominated as a member of the Rajya Sabha.

Marina Beach is so loooooong. I can never see the end of it on either side. Amma told me that it is the longest beach in the whole country! I simply love the sea. In the monsoon, when the sea gets quite rough, I am not allowed to get into the water. But I still love to go to Marina Beach, just to watch the huge waves, eat peanuts, enjoy the strong, cool breeze and run up and down the beach with Amma and Appa.

WATER, WATER, EVERYWHERE...
Three rivers run through Chennai: the Cooum River (also known as Triplicane River), the Adyar River and the Kosasthalaiyar River.

Did you know that there are many statues along Marina Beach? I cannot make out which statue is the tallest of them all. Can you? Actually, I just realized that there are a lot of statues all over Chennai! I don't think any another city in the country has so many statues of famous people.

SOME STATUES ON MARINA BEACH

Mahatma Gandhi

Netaji Subhas Chandra Bose

Kamaraj

Kannagi

Thiruvalluvar

Bharathiar

Dr Annie Beasant

G U Pope

Avvaiyar

There is also a fisherman's village on Marina Beach with a cute name — Nochchikuppam! Why don't you try and say it — Nochchi-kup-pam! Mala, my best friend, told me that her father buys the best fish from the fisherwomen at this village.

Once, during the monsoon, Mala and I watched a small fishing boat trying to come back to shore for more than half an hour. The sea was so rough. We both thought that the boat was going to topple over so many times, but it did not. We clapped so much when the boat safely reached the shore.

Mala's father had taken her to the Theosophical Society grounds in Adyar once. So, she asked our class teacher if we could all go there.

'There is a very huge banyan tree right in the middle of the grounds,' Ramya Ma'am said. 'Did you see that, Mala?'

'It is so huge!' Mala said, 'We can all play hide-and-seek there.'

On the last Friday of every month, our class teachers take us to some interesting spots in Chennai. So at the end of November, Mala got her wish and we all went off to Adyar. As soon as the school bus stopped, the whole class ran to the large banyan tree. All of us begged ma'am to let us play first. She agreed with a sigh. After a wonderful game of hide-and-seek, we were all very tired.

GUINDY NATIONAL PARK

It is one of the smallest national parks and one of the very few inside a city. It has blackbucks, spotted deer, civets, hyenas, pangolins, hedgehogs, mongooses, jackals, three-striped palm squirrels, a variety of snakes, tortoises, over 130 species of birds and over 60 species of butterflies.

Ramya Ma'am then took us all into the main hall and told us all about the great work that Annie Besant had done. She founded the Central Hindu School and College in Varanasi and started the Central Hindu School for Girls. The Indian Boy Scout Movement was also founded by her. And to top it all, she was elected President of the Indian National Congress. She wasn't even from India, she was from Great Britain! In 1907, she also became the President of the Theosophical Society.

THE THEOSOPHICAL SOCIETY

The Society was founded by Helena Petrovna Blavatsky and others in 1875. Its headquarters was moved from New York to Adyar in 1886. The large garden on the banks of the Adyar River is full of birds, fruit bats, snakes, jackals, wild cats, mongooses, hares, etc.

On the way back to school in the evening, you will never believe what we saw! Most of the class was fast asleep and suddenly we all were woken up with Ranga's voice shouting, 'Thalaivar! Thalaivar! Stop! Stop!'

The driver stopped as soon as he could on the side of the road and there was our famous Rajinikanth running on top of a bus! I will never forget it.

And, the weekend is here. Yay!

On Saturday, I slept till almost 8:30. I woke up to a very familiar aroma. Guess what it was — the aroma of yummy sambar and filter kaapi! Then I remembered, Saturday was Appa's Special Breakfast Day. I am sure that nobody else makes better dosas and sambar than my Appa. I ran to the kitchen. Amma was sitting on a chair, looking so sleepy. She was holding a davara of coffee.

'Amma!' I shouted, running to sit on her lap. 'Did you bring me presents from Delhi? And kaju barfi?'

'Aiiyyyoo!' Amma exclaimed, as she hugged me. 'Wait, kanna. You know I cannot think until I have had my coffee.'

SPECIAL FILTER KAAPI, PLEASE!

South Indian filter coffee is made by mixing boiling hot milk and the liquid obtained by brewing ground coffee powder in a stainless steel filter (percolator). The drink, known as Kaapi, is drunk from a stainless steel tumbler. It is often cooled first with a steel davara (bowl). This is done by pouring the coffee between the davara and the tumbler in huge arc-like movements of the hand.

Have you heard of one-metre coffee?

After Amma and Appa finished drinking their coffee, we decided to eat in the kitchen itself. Hot, hot dosas straight from the pan made with lots of ghee. Appa had made idlis for Amma. I don't like idlis much. I hope Appa makes vada sambar next Saturday. After breakfast, I had five pieces of kaju barfi!

In the afternoon, Appa helped me finish my math homework. Amma slept. The two days in Delhi for the conference had been very tiring, she said.

'Kutti,' said Appa suddenly, 'do you feel like watching a movie this evening?'

'Yes! Yes! Yes!' I shouted, and danced around the room, happy to get away from this math homework.

'So, finish your homework quickly!' he said, shattering my excitement.

Of course Amma woke up with all that shouting. But she had rested enough and she loves movies too. We took an auto and went to Devi Multiplex. Appa did not want to take the car because it is difficult to park there. We watched *Chennai Express.* It was a good movie. I especially loved all the songs in it.

We went to bed early because Amma wanted us all to go to the Cholamandal Artists' Village the next morning.

Everyone who lives in Cholamandal Artists' Village is an artist! There is an open-air theatre and everywhere we went, we saw sculptures of stone and metal. The museum and the gallery had so many paintings. I liked one painting very much. Amma also liked it.

'Look at how the artist has managed to show the power of the waves!' she exclaimed.

'That boat looks like it is going to be toppled by those huge waves!' I said.

Amma often tells me that she had started learning Carnatic vocal music when she was just six years old. I wish I could sing like her. I had also started learning at the same age, but I think Amma used to have less homework when she was my age. You should hear her singing 'Suprabhatam' — fantastic!

SA, RE, GA, MA, PA ...
The Music Academy, Madras, on TTK Road is very old and famous for the music festivals it has every winter. Everyone who loves Carnatic music tries to go for as many concerts as possible.

Amma's favourite singer is MS Subbulakshmi. Everyone calls her just MS. Imagine if I was known all over the country just as VS —Vijayalakshmi Srinivasan! But I guess I have to become as famous as MS first. Can you guess what MS stands for? Clue: M is the first letter of a large city in Tamil Nadu.

WHAT A VOICE!

Carnatic vocalist MS, or Madurai Shanmukhavadivu Subbulakshmi, was the first musician to be awarded the Bharat Ratna and the first Indian musician to receive the Ramon Magsaysay Award. Known as the Nightingale of India, she was also famous for the way she sang bhajans. She was awarded the Padma Bhushan and Padma Vibhushan too.

On Saturday morning, when I had a look at my calendar, I suddenly realized that Amma Paatti would be here in just two days. We will play Pallankuzhi and Dayakattai every day. I will sleep with her in her room. Every night she will tell me really funny stories about her childhood and I will help her buy saris for Chithi. I love my Amma Paatti so much!

But before that, there was something exciting planned for tonight too. We went for a night safari to the Crocodile Park with one of Appa's friends and his family. It was amazing! Did you know that the eyes of crocodiles look red at night? And they move quite fast too. There were hardly any lights on and we were given torch-lights to see the reptiles. It was so exciting! And, a little scary too. They even have Komodo Dragons there!

MCBT

The Madras Crocodile Bank Trust and Centre for Herpetology is the biggest crocodile sanctuary in India, located 40 km away from Chennai. It was set up by Romulus Whitaker. Now, there are more than 2,483 animals, including fourteen species of crocodiles, many species of turtles, snakes, etc.

On Sunday morning I practised making kolam designs. Kolams are usually made with dry rice flour (kolapodi). The powder is held in the hand, with a narrow gap between the thumb and the index finger to drop the rice powder in a straight line. I wish I could use a ruler.

There was a mother-and-daughter kolam competition in our colony and Amma and I got a Special Mention. It was a good thing that I had practised so much in the morning! You should have seen the winning kolam! It was so beautiful and perfect — an elephant with a peacock sitting on it!

Look at the difference between kolam and rangoli.

On Monday morning when I came back from school, Amma Paatti was already there! I did not let her sleep that afternoon and gave her all my news about Mala, the Crocodile Bank, Cholamandal, everything.

That evening Amma Paatti and I played Pallankuzhi for two hours. I won! Amma Paatti taught me how to play Dayakattai too. I really like the long dice that are used for this game. She carries her own set when she comes here. She says they are her lucky dice. Appa and Amma also played with us. Paatti taught me how to play Five Stones. Do you know how to play it?

GAME TIME!

Pallankuzhi is a game played by two players on a rectangular board with two rows and seven columns, 14 cups and 146 counters. Tamarind seeds or cowrie shells are used as coins.

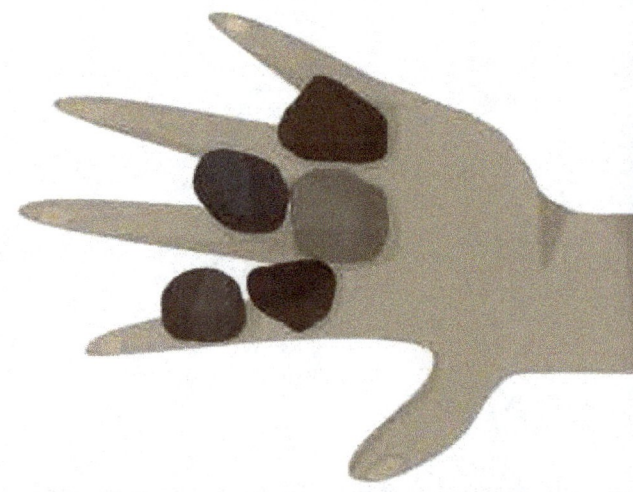

The next few weeks went so fast: dance practice, shopping, ordering food, deciding menus, more shopping and more dance practice. The Kanjeevaram saris were so beautiful. Amma Paatti let me chose two saris for Chithi. My favourite was bright red with a blue border.

KANJEEVARAM SILK SAREES
This world-famous woven silk is from Kanchipuram village in Tamil Nadu. They are very popular.

Just two days before the wedding, all my relatives arrived. Srini and Kamala Chithi arrived too. They looked so tired. Amma and Appa had taken ten days off from work. I had Christmas holidays, so I did not miss any classes in school. On the first day, many of my cousins just slept almost throughout the day because of jet lag. By the next day, they were all playing Dark Room, hide-and-seek and Antakshari. There was so much food being cooked in the kitchen all day. I am sure I saw more than 100 idlis the next morning on the dining table for breakfast!

I will never ever forget Kamala Chithi's wedding! She looked so beautiful in the Kalyana Mandapa. Srini looked very different in his dhoti. Amma and Appa gifted them a very big Nataraja statue.

That night we had a party at home. Srini and Kamla Chithi started the train dance and we all joined them, dancing through all the rooms in the house.

My arangetram was just one day after the wedding, so most of my relatives could watch me. I looked so grown up with all the make-up, jewellery and flowers. I think I made a slight mistake in the thillana in the end. After all the clapping, my cousin Kala from Boston came on the stage and hugged me. Radha Akka said she was very proud of me.

JUST IMAGINE!

The idol of Lord Nataraja in the Sri Nataraja Temple in Neyveli town, Cuddalore is the biggest in the world — 10 feet 1 inch tall!

Nataraja statues are usually handmade bronze sculptures cast by the artists using the lost wax process, a skill passed on for generations since the Chola period, depicting Shiva as the Lord of Dance. His dance is called Tandava.

Appa hired a mini-bus and we took all my cousins sightseeing. At Dakshina Chitra, we joined a terracotta clay class. I made a long wiggly snake. See! We watched a leather puppet show, did some block printing and even painted on cloth bags.

After that we all went to Elliot's Beach (named after Edward Elliot, who used to be the superintendent of police many years ago) for ice cream. We also visited Marina Beach, Kalakshetra, Theosophical Society and Amma's campus.

HOUSE ART IN CHENNAI

Dakshina Chitra has 18 historical houses. All these houses were bought, taken down very carefully, moved here and reconstructed exactly like they were first made! Even the exhibitions inside each of the houses are made to look as if people from the place where the house is from, still live inside.

Everyone finally left today; some in the morning, some in the afternoon and some in the evening. By the time I went to sleep, there were only Amma Paatti, Amma and Appa left in the house. The house was so quiet. Too quiet.

PLACES TO PRAY

Chennai and its suburbs have more than 600 temples! The oldest is the Parthasarathi Temple. The Kapaleeswarar Temple is dedicated to the Hindu god Shiva. Other places of worship are Luz Church, St Mary's Church, the San Thome Basilica, Wallajah Mosque and the Armenian Church of the Holy Virgin Mary.

POPULAR FESTIVALS

Pongal: A four-day long harvest festival celebrated in January. Before the festival, beautiful kolam designs are made at the entrance of homes.

Puthandu: This Tamil New Year takes place in mid-April. It is the beginning of the mango season and flowers of the neem tree also bloom at this time. People wear new clothes and eat maangapachadi, a dish made with mangoes, jaggery and neem flowers.

Golu: This is the festive display of dolls during the Dussehra festival. They are also called Bommai Kolu.

10 things to eat

1. Masala Dosa
2. Idli Sambar
3. Vada Sambar
4. Utthapam
5. Pongal
6. Chakli
7. Puli Saadam
8. Paalpayasam
9. Thaiyersadam
10. Kadale

10 things to do

1. Shop in Mylapore Market
2. Make sand castles at Elliot's Beach
3. Visit the Guindy National Park
4. Watch crocodiles at the Madras Crocodile Bank Trust and Centre for Herpetology
5. Visit the Arignar Anna Zoological Park
6. Take a trip to the Cholamandal Artists' Village
7. Learn to make a kolam design
8. Do jumping activities at Airborne Trampoline Park
9. Have fun at Qbowling
10. Solve mysteries at the Mystery Rooms

10 things to see

1. Fort St George
2. Government Museum
3. Valluvar Kottam
4. Gandhi Mandapam
5. Theosophical Society
6. Dakshina Chitra
7. Connemera Public Library
8. Marina Beach
9. Fishing Village
10. Kalakshetra Foundation

GLOSSARY

Aama: yes

Akka: older sister; also an informal term used for an elder female

Amma Paatti: mother's mother

Chithi: mother's sister

Illlay: no

Kanna: dear

Paatti: grandmother

Pavadai: long skirt

Po: go

Puu: flower

Thatha: grandfather

Vaa: come

Vanda: don't want

Thillana: usually the last part of the arangetram

OLDEST LANGUAGE

Tamil is a Dravidian language that is thought to be the oldest language still spoken in the world. It is an official language in three countries: India, Sri Lanka and Singapore. It is the official language of Tamil Nadu and the Union Territory of Puducherry. It is used as one of the languages of education in Malaysia, along with English, Malay and Mandarin.

About Indian National Trust for Art and Cultural Heritage (INTACH)

INTACH is a nationwide, non-profit membership organization to protect and conserve India's vast natural and cultural heritage. It is today the largest organization in the country dedicated to conservation. Heritage Education and Communication Service (HECS) of INTACH spreads awareness about India's natural, built, cultural, and living heritage. HECS promotes a love for heritage amongst children. It runs a network of heritage clubs. Each heritage club works on promoting the local culture and appreciating the rich diversity of India's heritage.

For further details, log on to: www. intach.org, www.youngintach.org

About Talking Cub

Talking Cub is the children's imprint of Speaking Tiger. Launched in December 2017, the imprint has published over thirty-five books, including those by renowned authors such as Ruskin Bond, Paro Anand, Ranjit Lal, Subhadra Sen Gupta, Deepa Agarwal and others. Some of the country's best fiction and non-fiction writing for children is part of the imprint. The details of all the titles can be seen at www.speakingtigerbooks.com.

Arthy Muthanna Singh is a children's writer, freelance journalist, copywriter, editor and cartoonist. She has a diverse range of experience in the publishing industry, a large part of it spent at *Limca Book of Records*. She has authored many books for children. She conducts creative writing workshops and dreams of moving to Goa some day.

Mamta Nainy is a children's writer based in New Delhi. She spent some years in advertising before an apple fell on her head while she was sitting under a mango tree, and she had her Eureka moment. She has been writing for children since then. She loves travelling but when she's too lazy to do it, she makes do with reading. She can usually be spotted next to a pile of children's books, chuckling to herself!

Vibha Surya is an independent illustrator based in Chennai. She has a Master's degree in Children's Literature & Illustration from Goldsmiths, University of London. She has worked with various advertising agencies, design studios and publishing companies. She's inspired by the people and places around her.